W9-DBH-325

HOW YOUR BODY WORKS

Fighting Diseases

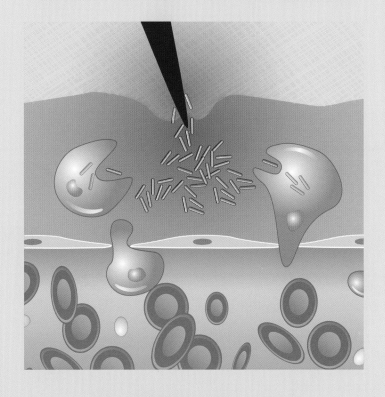

by Philip Morgan

amicus

Published by Amicus
P.O. Box 1329, Mankato, Minnesota 56002

Printed in the United States of America, at Corporate Graphics
in North Mankato, Minnesota

Library of Congress Cataloging-in-Publication Data
Morgan, Philip, 1948 Oct. 16-
  Fighting diseases / Philip Morgan.
      p. cm. -- (How your body works)
  Summary: "Discusses different diseases and disorders that affect the body,
and describes how the body responds to these illnesses"--Provided by publisher.
  Includes index.
  ISBN 978-1-60753-052-7 (library binding)
  1. Communicable diseases--Juvenile literature. I. Title.
  RC112.M66 2011
  616.9--dc22

                        2009047338

Created by Appleseed Editions Ltd.
Designed by Helen James
Edited by Mary-Jane Wilkins
Picture research by Su Alexander
Consultant: Steve Parker

Photograph acknowledgements
page 4 Randy Faris/Corbis; 5 Reuters/Corbis; 6 Tim Vernon, LTH NHS Trust/Science
Photo Library; 7 Bryan Reynolds/Science Faction/Corbis; 8 Clouds Hill Imaging Ltd/
Corbis; 9 Eye of Science/Science Photo Library; 10 Steve Gschmeissner/Science Photo
Library; 11 David Scharf/Science Faction/Corbis; 15 Ace Photo Agency/MedNet/Corbis;
16 Mark Clarke/Science Photo Library; 17 Eye of Science/Science Photo Library;
18 Michael Gabridge, Custom Medical Stock Photo/Science Photo Library; 22 T-Service/
Science Photo Library; 23 Ian Boddy/Science Photo Library; 24 Eye of Science/Science
Photo Library; 26 Howard Davies/Corbis; 27 C Goldsmith/Image Point FR/Corbis;
28 Bettmann/Corbis; 29 HBSS/Corbis
Front cover Eye of Science/Science Photo Library

DAD0037
32010

9 8 7 6 5 4 3 2 1

Contents

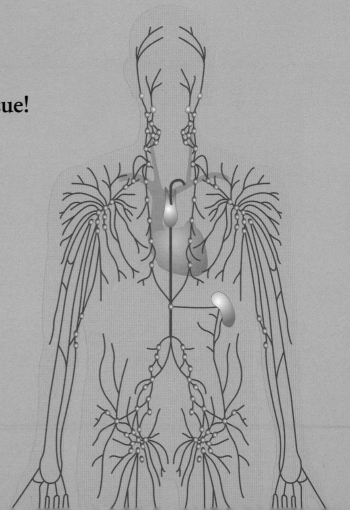

What Makes You Ill?

Most days you wake up with lots of energy. You feel good and eat a big breakfast. You're healthy, and although this sounds funny, you're "at ease" with your body. Then one day, you wake up with a runny nose, you sneeze a lot, feel tired, and ache in your joints. You look pale, have a headache, and feel hot all over. You don't feel like eating a thing.

What's Wrong?

You've probably caught an **infection**—you're no longer "at ease" with your body—in fact, you have a "dis-ease." You have

symptoms of the flu, or **influenza** to give it its full name. Your mom or dad gives you some medicine, which makes you feel a bit better. You'll probably have to stay in bed for a day or two while your body fights the disease, but then you'll be back on your feet and feeling better.

All Kinds of Diseases

The flu is just one of the diseases you can catch that make you ill. There are lots of others, such as colds, coughs, and eye and ear infections. More serious are infectious diseases such as **measles**, chicken pox, **rubella**, and **whooping cough**. Very serious infectious diseases include **meningitis**, **tuberculosis**, and **malaria**.

This book looks at infectious diseases and how your body defends itself against all the **microorganisms** that try to invade it. Not all diseases are caused by infections.

Taking your temperature is a good way to find out if you are ill.

These students wear masks to prevent catching a serious infectious disease.

Some people are born with diseases passed down to them from their parents. They can't fight them, so they have to live with them for their whole lives.

Diseases such as **arthritis** can be caused by something going wrong with your body. Sometimes drugs or surgery can help to relieve these diseases, but at other times people who have the disease have to learn to live with their illness.

Spanish Flu

After World War I, a deadly virus caused a disease called the Spanish flu. It spread around the world between 1918 and 1920, killing as many as 40 million people. Some people think that around 100 million died—this was 5 percent of the people in the world at that time.

Catching Diseases

Infectious diseases are caused by microorganisms. These might be **bacteria**, **viruses**, or **fungi**. They spread from person to person in different ways, such as coughing, sneezing, putting something infected in your mouth, or even sharing a toothbrush with someone who has an infectious disease.

Coughing sends a spray of droplets from your mouth. These may contain viruses or bacteria that cause disease.

Breathing In

You can catch some diseases by breathing in droplets that contain viruses. For example, the virus that causes flu is spread in tiny droplets of liquid that are coughed or sneezed into the air by someone who has the disease. If you breathe in and inhale those droplets into your lungs, the virus may enter your body. It might not give you the flu because your lungs may stop it from entering your bloodstream. If it does get into your blood, the virus begins to spread to the cells of your body where it grows, multiplies by the millions, and starts to mess up the way those cells work.

Swallowing Infection

Many infections enter your body through your mouth. If you drink infected water, the microorganisms in it can cause diseases in your digestive system. For example, water infected with tiny

A female mosquito can bite through your skin and suck out blood.

organisms called **amoebas** gives **diarrhea** to many children worldwide.

Organisms often get into water from the feces (waste) of infected people. An infection can spread from one person to another if they drink water that is polluted with sewage. This is why it is important that everyone in the world has clean water to drink. People can also carry organisms on their hands and fingers, which they may later put in their mouths. This is why it is important to wash your hands after you have been to the bathroom and before eating food.

Insect Bites

Some diseases can be spread by the bite of an insect. When an insect, such as a mosquito, bites your skin, a tiny drop of its saliva enters your blood. If the insect has already bitten someone who has a disease such as malaria, the organism enters your blood and you could catch the disease.

Did You Know?

Some foods can make you ill. Food can contain bacteria called salmonella. If foods such as chicken or shellfish are not cooked properly, they can cause food poisoning, which gives you diarrhea, fever, and vomiting.

Infections Everywhere

You can't sense the organisms that make you ill, but they are everywhere: in the air, in the soil, on door handles, in droplets, on carpets, in water—even on your skin and inside your digestive system! These organisms are called bacteria, viruses, and fungi.

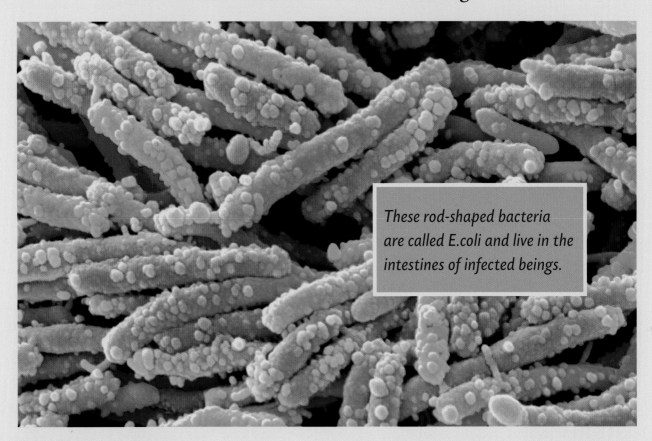

These rod-shaped bacteria are called E.coli and live in the intestines of infected beings.

Good and Bad

A bacterium is only a single cell, but there are many different kinds and they have different shapes, such as balls, rods, or spirals. Some are harmful and cause diseases, although most don't. In fact, many bacteria are essential because they recycle the atoms and molecules of the world. But bacteria can cause some very serious infectious diseases. These include tetanus (lockjaw), typhoid fever, **leprosy**, tuberculosis, and **cholera**.

Vile Viruses

Viruses are very different from bacteria. They are tiny—100 times smaller than bacteria—and they are **parasites**. This means they can't live on their

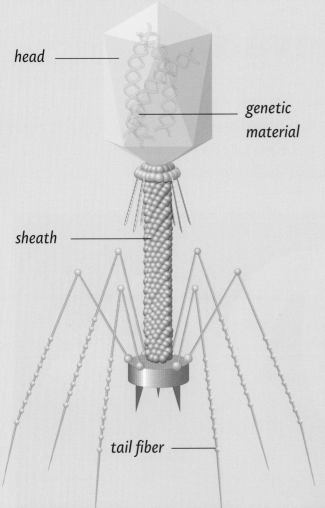

head

genetic material

sheath

tail fiber

This virus looks like a rocket with landing legs. It is not harmful to people, but it attacks bacteria by injecting them.

and intestines, as well as on patches of sore skin. Usually thrush doesn't cause problems, but sometimes it grows out of control and makes a white liquid, which makes people itch.

own, but need the cells of other organisms, such as you, to grow and reproduce. Not all viruses cause diseases, but a lot do—and they can be nasty! Chicken pox, flu, colds, polio, **yellow fever**, HIV/AIDS, and **hepatitis** B are all caused by viruses.

Fungi Make You Itch!

The fungi that cause infections are tiny organisms that infect your skin, nails, scalp, and eyes, and make them itchy or irritated. One is like the yeast used to make bread rise. Its name is thrush (or candida), and it lives in the mouth

THE FUNGUS THAT SOUNDS LIKE A WORM

Ringworm is a fungus that causes a ring-shaped reddish patch of skin. Ringworm often infects feet, especially the warm, damp skin between the toes. This type of ringworm is called athlete's foot.

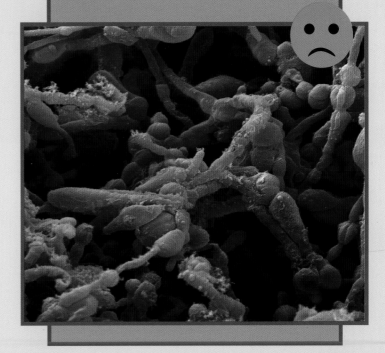

Animal Invaders

Tiny animals can invade our bodies. These invaders are called parasites and they are usually a type of worm or tiny animal that is made of just one cell. These invaders can make us feel very ill.

Wicked Worms

There are two types of worms that find their way into our bodies: roundworms and flatworms. Worms that get into your digestive system usually cause problems with the intestines. Worms in the lungs can give people coughs and fevers. The only way to get rid of them is to take medicine prescribed by a doctor.

The pinworm is a common roundworm. The worm's eggs may be in house dust, or can be swallowed in food, or get onto people's fingers. The eggs hatch into worms inside the intestines. At night, the females lay eggs around the anus, which makes it very itchy. Scratching the itch means the eggs can get on your fingers, which might spread them to other people.

This pinworm can live in people's intestines. It is also called a threadworm or a roundworm.

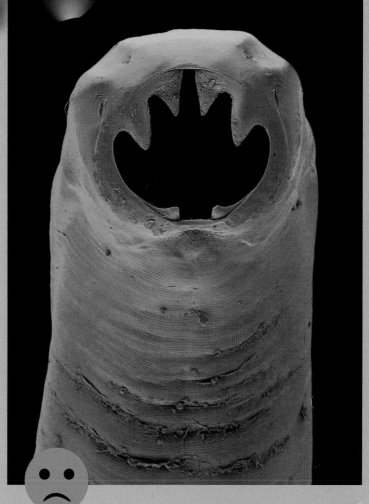

This hookworm lives in the small intestine. Hookworms can cause problems because they suck blood from the wall of the intestines.

Small but Deadly

Tiny organisms with just one cell are called **protozoa**. They can give people some of the worst diseases. A disease called malaria is caused by one of them. This organism gets into people's blood when a type of female mosquito bites them. The most deadly type kills millions of people every year, mostly children who live in warm, wet parts of the world. In some countries, the drinking water may contain another protozoan that causes bad diarrhea and makes people feel very ill.

Defending Your Body

Your body has several defenses that help keep out bacteria, viruses, and other organisms that might make you ill. Your skin keeps most things out and the main places that organisms can get into your body are through your mouth, eyes, nose, and ears.

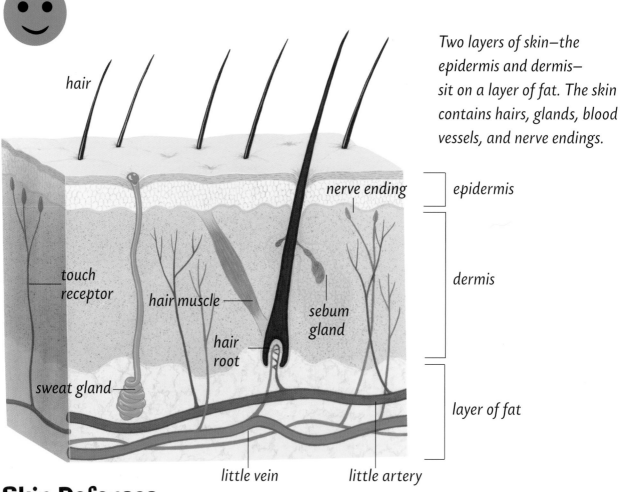

Two layers of skin—the epidermis and dermis—sit on a layer of fat. The skin contains hairs, glands, blood vessels, and nerve endings.

hair

nerve ending

epidermis

touch receptor

hair muscle

dermis

sebum gland

hair root

sweat gland

layer of fat

little vein

little artery

Skin Defenses

Glands in your skin produce an oily, waxy substance called **sebum**. This keeps your skin smooth and waterproof, and protects against bacteria. The glands are beside the hairs on your skin. Sweat also has a mild chemical that helps to kill bacteria. When you cut yourself, a scab quickly forms on your skin. The scab stops **germs** from getting into your blood. If bacteria get into a cut, it becomes infected and oozes pus. Chemicals called antiseptics can stop this from happening by killing the bacteria.

Glands Versus Bacteria

We all have glands in our mouths that produce slimy saliva and mucus that kill organisms. At the back of your nose and throat are glands called **tonsils** and **adenoids**. They are very good at trapping and killing bacteria. If your tonsils are infected with germs, you have tonsillitis.

ACID IN THE STOMACH

Tiny glands in the lining of your stomach make a strong chemical called hydrochloric acid. Usually this acid helps to break down food, but it is also very good at killing organisms that might give you diseases if they manage to get past your mouth.

Did You Know?

If your eyes are infected by bacteria or viruses, then you have pink eye, or conjunctivitis. You can also develop this itchy condition if your eyes are irritated by smoke or pollution, or if you have an allergy.

Tears are made in lacrimal glands above the eyes and drain away in tear ducts at the corner.

Healthy Eyes

Your eyes have two defenses—tears and eyelashes. Eyelashes stop tiny bits of dust and grit from entering your eyes. Your eyes are washed all the time with tears that contain a bit of salt and a chemical that kills bacteria. You have glands behind your eyes that make a constant supply of these tears.

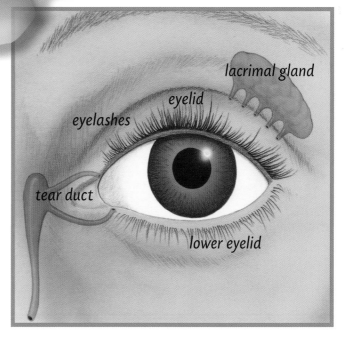

lacrimal gland
eyelid
eyelashes
tear duct
lower eyelid

Spots and Rashes

Your skin is your body's first defense against infection. Spots and rashes on your skin can be a sign that something is wrong and that your body is trying to fight off invaders. The spots might be itchy or sore, and you may feel generally unwell, too.

Oily Skin

Sometimes the glands in your skin produce too much oily sebum. This can happen when you become a teenager. The sebum clogs up the hair follicles and then turns hard and black. This is how blackheads are formed. They are a form of acne, which appears mainly on the face and upper body. Bacteria infect blackheads and make the skin around them red and sore. Teenagers also get other sorts of acne called whiteheads, or red pimples that fill with pus when bacteria get inside. It's important to keep skin as clean as possible with soap and water and to never squeeze an acne blemish.

Chicken Pox and Measles

Two common infections that cause rashes are chicken pox and measles. You catch both by breathing in infected droplets from the air. The good news is that once you have had them, you are **immune** to

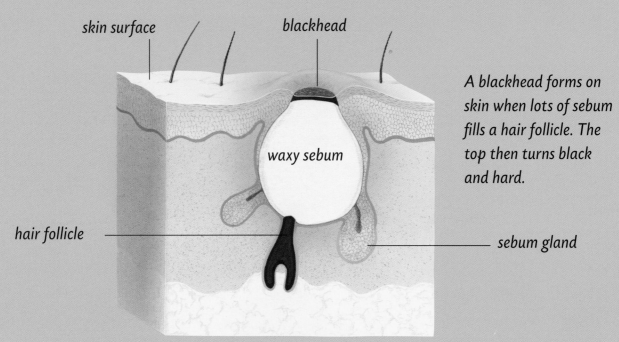

skin surface   blackhead

waxy sebum

hair follicle

sebum gland

A blackhead forms on skin when lots of sebum fills a hair follicle. The top then turns black and hard.

the viruses. This means that you'll never catch them again.

When you have chicken pox, you feel as though you have flu, and you have a rash of tiny red spots on your skin—in one place or all over your body. The spots fill with liquid and look like blisters—they are very itchy. Anyone who touches them can catch the virus.

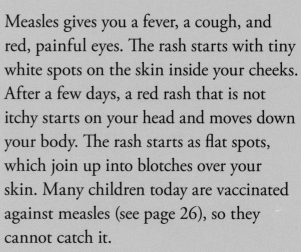

WHEN THINGS GO WRONG

Boils and Stys
If a hair follicle is infected with bacteria, it can turn into a boil. If it is an eyelash, the boil is called a sty. As a boil grows, it has a head, which is white or yellow. Then it might burst or heal on its own without bursting.

Measles gives you a fever, a cough, and red, painful eyes. The rash starts with tiny white spots on the skin inside your cheeks. After a few days, a red rash that is not itchy starts on your head and moves down your body. The rash starts as flat spots, which join up into blotches over your skin. Many children today are vaccinated against measles (see page 26), so they cannot catch it.

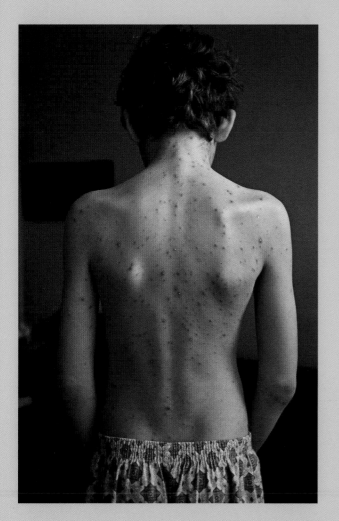

This boy has chicken pox. The tiny red spots all over his back fill with liquid and can be very itchy.

Annoying Allergies

Your body is surrounded by chemicals, pollen, and dust.
Usually they are harmless and don't have any effect on you.
But sometimes your body overreacts to one of them.
This happens when you have an allergy—and allergies can be
very annoying, as anyone who suffers from them knows.

*Pollen produced by flowers
can cause hay fever.*

Your Body Fights Back

Something that triggers an allergy is
called an allergen. Many things can
become an allergen: it may be chemicals
in your food, in water, or in the air, pollen
from grasses or flowers, dust, insect stings,
and even some medications. Your body
treats allergens as invaders and attacks
them with its immune system (see page
24). The first contact with an allergen
triggers your immune system so that
when the allergen returns, the system
will respond with an allergic reaction.

These are what pollen grains from grass look like under a microscope.

Bad Reaction

There are cells in your skin, the lining of your nose, and in other tissues called mast cells. These cells contain a chemical called histamine. When you have an allergic reaction, the mast cells are destroyed and histamine enters the tissues. This is what causes your symptoms.

There are many allergies, and each one has its own symptoms. Hay fever causes sneezing and itchy eyes, nose, and throat. An allergy to cow's milk causes diarrhea and vomiting. Some illnesses can involve an allergic reaction, such as asthma, which can be triggered by house dust mites. The itching skin of eczema can be related to an allergy to a particular food.

Allergies Can Be Triggered By:

Touching Skin
animal scratch, poisonous plant, pollen

Breathing In
pollen, animal skin or hair, mold, mildew, dust, dust mites

Bites and Stings
bee, wasp, mosquito

Eating
nuts, shellfish

Inside Your Air Passages

Viruses and bacteria can attack the air passages through which you breathe. They may cause problems in the lining of your windpipe or deep inside your lungs, as well as in the **sinuses** in your face. They can give you colds, coughs, sore throats, and other illnesses.

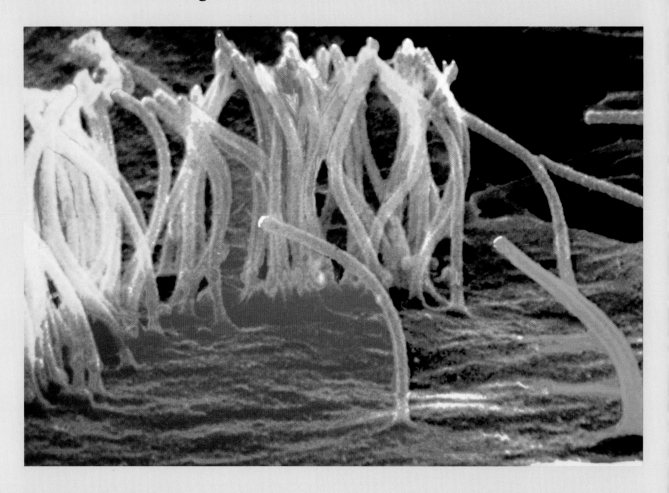

Bacteria Traps

The lining of your air passages makes a slimy liquid called mucus, which traps bacteria and particles such as pollen and dust. Your lungs also have thousands of tiny hairs called cilia. These work together to move mucus up to the top

Tiny hairs called cilia grow on the lining of the airways in your lungs.

of the windpipe, or trachea, and into your throat. Here, the mucus is either swallowed or moved into your mouth when you clear your throat.

Catching a Cold

Viruses give you colds. There are probably hundreds of different cold viruses, so you'll never catch them all in your lifetime. You catch them from the coughs and sneezes of people who are already infected. When you catch a cold, the lining of your air passages and your sinuses (the spaces connected to your nose inside the front of your skull) make lots of mucus and start to swell. Thick mucus is called phlegm (say "flem") or catarrh (say "cat-ar"). For a while you sneeze, cough, and your nose may run as mucus drips out of it.

A bronchus is one of the airways that branch off the windpipe in your lungs. You have bronchitis if bacteria infect the lining of the airway. Its wall thickens and your lungs make lots of mucus.

More Than a Cold

If phlegm turns yellowish-green, it may be infected with bacteria. Doctors call this a secondary infection. It is a sign that the cold has moved down to your chest. This can cause bronchitis. If this happens, the insides of your lungs become inflamed (see page 20) and produce huge amounts of mucus. This narrows the air passages and makes breathing difficult.

normal bronchus

bronchus with bronchitis

The Big Fight

Once an organism that causes disease breaks through your body's defenses, it comes face to face with your tissues. These include your blood and the mucus membranes that line your body's passageways and cover your tissues. Your body's first —and fastest—response to this invasion is **inflammation**.

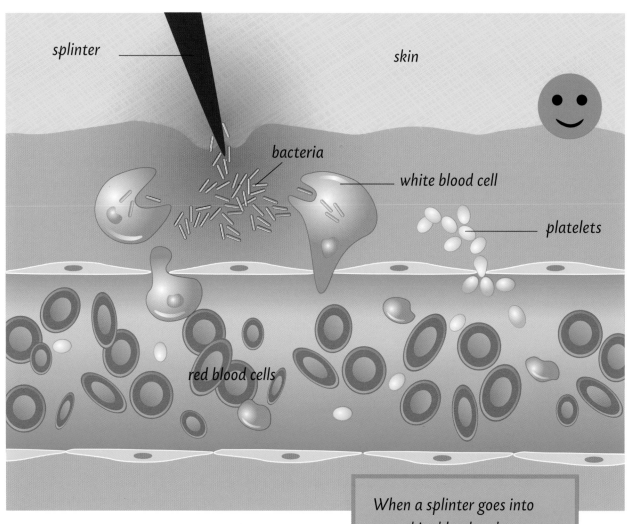

splinter

skin

bacteria

white blood cell

platelets

red blood cells

When a splinter goes into your skin, blood rushes to the place to heal the wound.

Blood to the Rescue

Inflammation has four stages: redness, heat, swelling, and pain. Imagine you fall over and bang your knee. Your body rushes more blood to the knee, which makes it look red and heats it up. White blood cells (see page 24) attack any bacteria that enter the wound. The knee swells up and you feel pain—this is a reminder that you've hurt yourself and should take care of the injured place.

A Pocket of Pus

The fight against invading bacteria can be messy. White blood cells battle with bacteria where they have caused infection. There are usually a lot of casualties—many bacteria, white cells, and cells in the body's tissue die. They collect together in a pocket of pus, called an abscess, which is usually a thick, greenish-yellow liquid.

As the abscess grows, it pushes on the surrounding tissues. This makes the area swollen and painful. If the body loses the fight against the bacteria, a doctor might need to prescribe antibiotics (see page 28) to kill the bacteria and drain the abscess.

Bacteria can infect the soft center, or pulp, of a tooth. When they move down to the root, lots of pus is produced and a painful abscess forms.

Toothache

The bacteria inside your mouth love sugar. They break it down into an acid, which dissolves the enamel on the outside of your teeth and can eventually reach the layer of dentine inside the teeth. That's when problems start.

The bacteria invade the pulp at the core of the tooth, causing serious toothache. Eventually, bacteria and poisons from the decaying pulp reach the root of the tooth and form a pus-filled abscess. If a dentist can treat the abscess in time, the tooth may be saved, otherwise it has to be pulled.

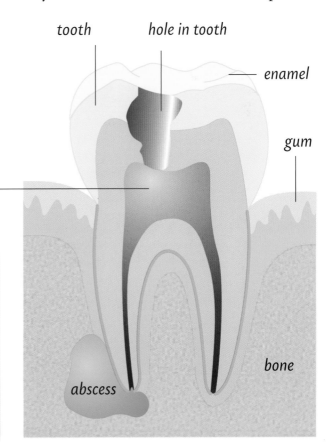

tooth   *hole in tooth*

— enamel

gum

infected pulp —

bone

abscess

The Heat of the Battle

When you are well, your body temperature is steady,
even when the weather is very cold or boiling hot. But when
you are fighting an infection caused by bacteria or viruses,
your temperature rises because you develop a fever.

Not too Hot, Not too Cold

Usually, your blood keeps the temperature of your body under control. When it's cold outside, the blood vessels in your skin narrow and your hairs stand on end, giving you goose bumps. This stops your body from losing heat. When you move around, your muscles create heat, which also warms you.

The orange and yellow areas shown on these men are losing heat fastest.

Brrrrrr!

To find out how the body responds to extreme cold, medical scientists have lowered people's body temperature to between 70°F and 75°F (21°C and 24°C). Normal body temperature is 98.6°F (37°C). They found that very cold people breathe very slowly and their hearts beat very slowly, too. They may lose consciousness, but surprisingly their cells or tissues are not damaged when their bodies return to a normal temperature.

Medicine can lower the temperature of someone with a fever.

The opposite happens when your body becomes too hot. The blood vessels widen so that when the blood reaches your skin, it cools a little and the skin reddens. Sweat glands in your skin produce more sweat than normal. As this evaporates into the air, your skin cools.

Several diseases cause fevers, including scarlet fever, yellow fever, and glandular fever. If your temperature rises as high as 104°F (40°C), the fever can become dangerous and you may need to seek emergency medical care.

HEALTH CHECK
Taking your Temperature

Your body temperature is usually 98.6°F (37°C). If you feel ill, your parents may take your temperature by putting a thermometer under your tongue. If your temperature is 100°F (38°C) or more, then you have a fever. Fevers are part of the body's normal reaction to infection, so there is usually nothing to worry about.

Blood Cells to the Rescue!

When a microorganism gets past the body's defenses
and invades your blood, your body fights it with
a very clever system. This is your immune system.
It has different cells that work in your bloodstream
as well as in a network of other channels.

Your immune system recognizes an invading organism right away. When the system detects an invader, it immediately attacks, fights it, and tries to get rid of it.

Many of the symptoms you have when you are ill, such as a high temperature, are the result of this fight. Usually the cells in your immune system succeed in fighting off the invader.

Weapons Against Disease

Your immune system uses several weapons to fight disease. When an invader damages a tissue in your body, the tissue becomes inflamed (see pages 20–21). It swells and turns red, releasing chemicals into

your blood. These act as messengers that call for help and alert various types of white blood cells to come rushing to the rescue.

Large white blood cells called phagocytes (say "fago-sites") hunt down the invaders and gobble them up if they can.

This white blood cell is part of the body's immune system.

24

The invaders that are not gobbled up are then attacked by lymphocytes (say "lim-fo-sites"), another type of white blood cell. These cells can identify the chemicals the invader is made of and produce their own substances to attack it.

In particular, lymphocytes attack invading organisms by making substances called antibodies to kill or disable them. Some lymphocytes remember a particular invader. So if it returns, the lymphocytes will be ready to attack it.

All Around the Body

Your lymph system reaches many parts of your body and links tissues such as the tonsils, adenoids, **thymus gland**, and **spleen**. It filters fluid from all your tissues and returns clean fluid to your blood.

The system carries a clear fluid called lymph. The filtering places are called lymph nodes, where phagocytes engulf invaders. The nodes are where your body makes more phagocytes and lymphocytes to fight off an invading organism.

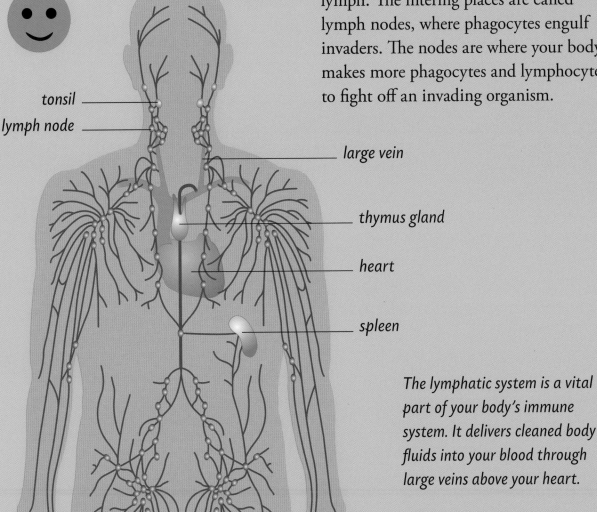

tonsil

lymph node

large vein

thymus gland

heart

spleen

The lymphatic system is a vital part of your body's immune system. It delivers cleaned body fluids into your blood through large veins above your heart.

Stopping Disease

Smallpox, polio, and tuberculosis killed many people during the nineteenth century. Since then, doctors have searched for ways to control the spread of fatal diseases. If we can educate people on disease prevention, we can stop disease in its tracks and stop it from spreading.

Triggering Defenses

Medical scientists and doctors make vaccines to prevent people from catching some serious diseases. They use their knowledge of the way white blood cells called lymphocytes remember viruses to help them. Today, vaccinations can help to protect, or immunize, your body against some diseases.

A vaccine triggers your immune system to make antibodies, which work against a virus even if the living virus is not in your body. In other words, if you have a measles vaccination, you will never catch measles—you can be protected from it without having the illness itself.

Victory Against Smallpox

Smallpox is a very infectious disease that causes reddish blisters on people's faces, arms, and legs. It was so deadly in the 1700s that it killed hundreds of thousands of people every year. In 1796, an English doctor named Edward Jenner discovered how to make a vaccine from

A health care worker vaccinates a Rwandan child against measles.

Changing Viruses

Some of the viruses that make you ill—for example, the viruses which give you a cold, influenza (flu), or AIDS—keep changing into new types of viruses. As a result, your body is unable to recognize them, so you keep having these illnesses. Doctors cannot develop vaccines against this sort of illness.

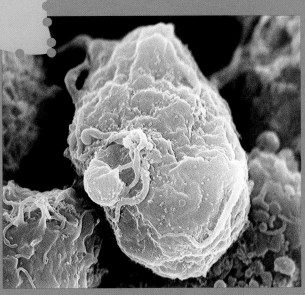

HIV, the virus that causes AIDS, sits on a lymphocyte.

cows who had caught a similar disease known as cowpox. Since 1980, after a vaccination program around the world, no one has caught smallpox and it is the first serious infectious disease to be wiped out altogether.

HEALTH CHECK
Protecting Against Disease

People all over the world receive vaccinations to help protect them from serious diseases. Most babies and young children are given a vaccine called MMR which stops them from catching measles, **mumps**, and rubella. If you travel abroad to places where there may be dangerous organisms in the drinking water, you can have a vaccine to protect you against typhoid fever. This is a deadly disease caused by bacteria called salmonella.

Taking Medicine

When you are ill, you may need treatment to help you fight the disease you have. For centuries, doctors treated sick people with medicines and remedies that were made from natural ingredients such as herbs. Just over a hundred years ago, scientists began to use artificial drugs to make pills, and these fought against disease more effectively.

Aches and Pains

When you are ill, you may have a headache, pain, and a fever—all common symptoms of illness. Many people take aspirin or acetaminophen tablets to help themselves feel better. These drugs are called **painkillers**. Aspirin was one of the first drugs to be made. It lowers the body's temperature and takes away pain. Acetaminophen takes away aches and pains, too, and can also bring down a high temperature and reduce inflammation.

Killing Bacteria

In 1928, a Scottish scientist named Alexander Fleming discovered penicillin, which he made from a fungus. This drug was one of the first powerful antibiotics, which are drugs that kill bacteria. Antibiotics don't kill viruses, so they have no effect on illnesses such as colds, flu, or AIDS.

Alexander Fleming looks down a microscope in his laboratory.

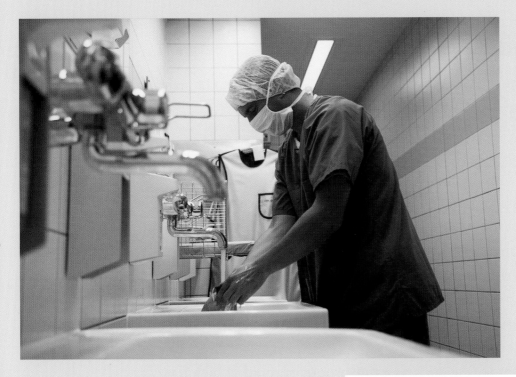

A surgeon washes his hands so he doesn't take any germs into the operating room.

Penicillin saved many people's lives during World War II because it stopped people from dying from infected wounds. Soon the search was on to find other fungi that could be used to make antibiotics. Today, doctors have a wide range of antibiotics to choose from, so many diseases are no longer as dangerous as they once were.

Did You Know?

Today some bacteria have found a way of resisting the power of antibiotics that once killed them. Sometimes doctors have to prescribe a different antibiotic in order to kill them.

HOSPITAL INFECTIONS

Deadly infections can attack hospital patients. One called MRSA resists nearly every antibiotic. Some people carry MRSA bacteria in their noses or on their skin and don't become ill. If the bacteria get inside the body or into the blood, they can cause infections. This may be dangerous for people who are ill in the hospital. The bacteria are spread by touch, so it is important that everyone in a hospital washes their hands often and thoroughly.

Glossary

adenoids   Small lumps of lymph tissue at the lower back of the nose.

AIDS   A disease caused by a virus called HIV, which affects the body's immune system.

amoeba   A type of microorganism with one cell. Some amoebae cause serious diseases of the digestive system.

arthritis   A disease that makes joints painful and stiff.

bacteria   A huge group of microorganisms with one cell. Only a few types of bacteria cause serious diseases.

cholera   An infection caught by eating or drinking infected food or water, allowing bacteria into the small intestine.

diarrhea   A stomach and intestine illness that makes your feces (waste) more liquid than usual.

fungus   A living organism such as a mushroom or mold, which has no flowers or leaves and obtains food by growing on other organisms.

germs   A name for organisms that invade your body and cause disease and illness.

gland   An organ in your body that makes a substance or a chemical.

hepatitis   An illness of the liver that is caused by viruses.

immune   If you are immune to a disease, your body can fight it off without feeling ill.

infection   A disease caused by an organism that invades your body.

inflammation   Painful redness or swelling of parts of your body caused by an organism, an injury, or an irritant.

influenza   An infection in the upper part of the lungs caused by a virus.

leprosy   An infection of the skin and nerves caused by bacteria.

malaria   An infection of the red blood cells caused by a protozoan.

measles   A childhood illness in which a virus causes a rash and a fever.

meningitis   An infection of the layers that cover the brain and spinal cord. Meningitis may be caused by a virus or a bacterium.

microorganisms   Tiny, or microscopic, organisms such as bacteria, viruses, protozoa, and some fungi.

mumps   A viral infection that makes your salivary glands swell.

parasites   Organisms that live off other hosts, like human beings.

protozoa   A group of single-celled organisms, such as an amoeba.

rubella   An infectious disease that causes a rash.

sebum   A waxy substance produced by glands in the skin.

sinus   An air space at the front of the skull.

spleen   An organ that breaks down red blood cells and makes white blood cells.

thymus gland   An organ that produces white blood cells.

tonsils   Areas of lymph tissue at the back of your throat on either side.

tuberculosis   A bacterial infection that usually affects the lungs.

viruses   Organisms that cause infection and can only reproduce inside living cells.

whooping cough   A bacterial infection of the windpipe and airways.

yellow fever   A viral infection that may turn the body yellow.

Books

Brownlee, Christen. *Cute, Furry, and Deadly: Diseases You Can Catch From Your Pet!* Franklin Watts, 2008.

Denshire, Jayne. *Hygiene (Healthy Habits)*. Smart Apple Media, 2011.

Schaefer, A.R. *Staying Healthy*. Heinemann Library, 2010.

Watson, Stephanie. *Superbugs: The Rise of Drug-Resistant Germs*. Rosen Publishing, 2010.

Web Sites

http://kidshealth.org/kid/ill_injure/index.html
Find out about all kinds of illnesses, from flu
and chicken pox to tonsillitis and pin worms.

http://www.cdc.gov/DiseasesConditions/
Visit the U.S. Centers for Disease Control and Prevention web
page and learn about current diseases affecting people worldwide.

Index

abscess   21
acne   14
adenoids   13, 25
AIDS   9, 27, 28
allergy   13, 16–17
amoeba   7
analgesics   28
antibiotics   21, 28–29
antibodies   25, 26
asthma   17

bacteria   6, 7, 8, 9, 12, 13,
    14, 15, 18, 19, 21, 22,
    25, 27, 28, 29
bronchitis   19

chicken pox   4, 9, 14, 15
cholera   8
colds   4, 9, 18, 19, 27, 28
coughs   4, 6, 10, 15, 18,
    19

defenses   12, 13, 14, 20,
    24, 26
diarrhea   7, 11, 17

fever   7, 10, 15, 22, 23, 28
flu   4, 5, 6, 9, 27, 28

germs   12, 29
glands   12, 13, 14, 23

hay fever   16, 17
hepatitis   9

immune system   16,
    24–25, 26
infection   4, 6, 8, 9, 14,
    19, 21, 22, 23, 29
inflammation   20–21,
    24, 28
insect bites   7, 17
intestines   8, 9, 10, 11

leprosy   8
lungs   6, 10, 18–19
lymph system   25

malaria   4, 7, 11
measles   4, 14, 15, 26,
    27
meningitis   4
microorganisms   6, 24
mosquito   7, 11
mucus   18–19
mumps   27

pain   20, 21, 28
parasite   8, 10
penicillin   28–29
polio   9, 26
proteins   25
pus   12, 14, 21

rashes   14–15
ringworm   9
rubella   4, 27

salmonella   7, 27
sebum   12, 14
sinuses   18, 19
skin   9, 12, 14, 17, 20, 23
smallpox   26–27
sneezing   6, 17, 19
spleen   25
stings   16, 17
sty   15

temperature   4, 22–23,
    24, 28
thymus gland   25
tonsils   13, 25
toothache   21
tuberculosis   4, 8, 26

vaccination   15, 26–27
viruses   6, 8, 9, 12, 13, 15,
    18, 19, 22, 25, 26, 27, 28

white blood cells   20, 21,
    24, 25, 26
whooping cough   4
worms   10–11

yellow fever   9, 23